Island Bound Mail

Island Bound Mail

Poems by

Nancy Anne Miller

Kelsay Books

Cover art: *Semitropical Letters*, Collage, Nancy Anne Miller

ISBN: 13-978-1-945752-98-8

Kelsay Books
Aldrich Press
www.kelsaybooks.com

For Evie, May, Rita, who raised me up

Acknowledgments

Ber-News: "Bermuda Google Earth"

The Country and Abroad: "I Is for Immigrant," "House Visit," "Hot Water Bottle," "Lockets," "Rocking the Fixer," "Island Bound Mail"

Interviewing the Caribbean: "What is Shade," "How to Dress for a Funeral," "Un-Box"

A New Ulster: "Falling in Love with my Father in the Snow," "Island Bound Mail," "I Re-Member," "Bermuda Land Snail," "Rock Solid," "Sea Pudding," "Crime Scene"

Metaphor: "Film Strip"

The Missing Slate: "Lockets"

Papercuts: "Painted Woman"

Poems of Pacuare Anthology: "Camel"

Poui: "Seduction," "I Is for immigrant," "House Visit," "Hot Water Bottle," "Flight Attendant," "Shakespearean"

Words on Waves Anthology 2016: "Rocking the Fixer"

Contents

Searching for the Bermuda Triangle

The Peril of Politeness

Plankton

Times Squared

Poetry is news that stays news.

—Ezra Pound

Searching for the Bermuda Triangle

I Is for Immigrant

The vertical you become
leaving your country.

I is for how you see
differently, eye pupils learn

another country. I is for
I'm a migrant now. I is

for the two stitches sewn
across a border, top one

holds the fray of exit,
bottom, the pull of return.

House Visit

Cousin Tina tells me I can have my pick
of china pieces on a mahogany table.
They rise like rose corals, stuck to
a reef. The house now has a deep

sea feel, shafts of light bounce
off of mirrors, surf crashes and
slipcovers, bureaus are stripped
of buttons, handles as if an interior

life no longer exists, everything open,
up for grabs. As if currents rushed
through, left books, drawers on floors.
My great Aunt Susie took tea in the side

garden. Harriet carrying the tray of
silver, a game of chess where each
part is thoughtfully placed. I remember
the rough image of *Pearl,* the lost

family ship, etched into the side
of the house, a child's finger drawing
or one drawn in sand by a stick, the ocean
removes layer by layer as it polishes

the sand into the sheen of a tidy
housekeeper. Each ruffle of tide
luminous as a shell, where grit spins
into a jewel deep inside an oyster.

Island Bound Mail

The sign at the Post Office
shows what a terrorist
package might look like.

Just like the one I send,
has a clump of stamps in
the shape of Matisse's Snail.

A school of fish swims
the front, headed up
for the surface. Bits of

Scotch tape here, there,
like a snapper scaled.
And the loose brown

package paper, a sweater
a sibling hands down
to you, big, baggy,

the Shetland Wool
unravels into the string
wound round and round.

The postmistress asks if
anything is explosive
inside. I want to say, *Yes!*

Books have been known
to cause revolutions, pages
turning, fan many a fire!

The non-terrorist package
has the US Postal Eagle.
Swift, eyes anything out

of uniform, what strays across
lines, roams 3rd class mail, it
is eager to pick up in tallows.

Rock Solid

Bermudians don't need rocking chairs
to cool out, relax. The ocean will do
with the tide quick-sanding the beach,
leaving while arriving, such a sway of water.

Bermudians remember the hand steadies
the boat slapping up to the dock, like
a pup to a bitch's teat, jumps up in the air.
Bermudians need a solid chair while they

watch the horizon where waves rise up
like children to peek over the flat line fence,
to see what is beyond. No need to tilt
back, forth, bringing it in, out of focus.

Look, Look, Don't Look!

Look, look, don't look!
The shark's come in too close,
driving for the display of blood,
a bull for a vivid cape.

Look, look, don't look!
The man's gone out too far,
might cut, might cut, don't say
might cut, might spoil his time.

Look, look, don't look!
Over the picnic aunties,
comes *help! help! help!*
someone's in Hell.

Look, look, don't look!
Move away up from the beach,
go home children to your beds,
may the dark cover your sleep.

Look, look, don't see!
The body blots the beach,
Went out too far, don't say
might cut, don't spoil his time.

Film Strip

I don't know how to think
about film now it is digital.
Before, there was a strip of

negatives, a train shuttles by.
The reel turned like a conch
inwards, the last clips from

the canister drooped, a dog's
tail curls between legs.
The projector streamed its

flashlight, guided the army
of beige seats, uniformed in
the dark. The outdoor movie

screen at Coral Beach blew
away, a sail into the sea,
while I gasped as the night

descended on families
watching, left us alone to
work out where our stories

begin. While the waves
broke on the beach with
a hushed rush of applause.

I Re-Member

Like a candle streaming light onto
the page, my fountain pen leaks
Turquoise ink as I write about my isle.

I remember College Weeks when youth
buzzed the island in hummingbird flocks.
Left heaps of Mobylettes on Front Street

with handlebars, gears, and bicycle chains
enmeshed in group sex. I re-member
the sail's envelope flap in the harbor

where the waves rose up in tips below,
the sea's letter written out in long
hand we learned at Bermuda High School

for Girls. I remember shoving handfuls
of Crow Lane's Banana bread in my mouth
after school, ingesting the island's moist

soil. I remember the light sugar
cubed in limestone blocks, chalky,
made houses brim, float like a poem,

the white washed roofs ascending,
as Emily Dickinson said of poetry:
the top of her head taken off.

Seduction

The roots of the screw palm
look like group sex, legs
bonking into other legs.

The wind rustles the crinoline
of palm leaves pulled up
by the hands of a coquettish

woman. The hibiscus kiss
the day with their red, red
lipstick, blot it with a curvy

mouth. The elephant plant
drops a large ear, drags it along
the ground, wants to hear

the gossip. The tourists want
to catch the sun, tossed like
a Frisbee by skittish wind back,

forth through clouds. The visitors
want to hold its gold ring now after
the merry go round of seasons.

Long limbed as a chorus girl,
makes a late day entrance,
sequined with rain, kicking.

Sea Pudding

That the sea would bake one, create a caramel
sponge, spotted as Pauline's, our cook's face,
her light brown skin dotted with moles.

Soft as the bodies of black woman, who
took care of us Colonial Girls. May sewing
Liberty of London dresses for Cissette,

and Wendy, my Madame Alexander Dolls.
Rita ironing shirts, transformed them
from a gloppy jelly fish substance, stiffened

with the backbone of starch, while I
pestered her with questions. Evie cleaning
my privates as I sat in the tub, asking if

I had any company? The shock America
was for me as teenagers babysat children,
picked them up, put them down casually

as a plastic toy. *Isochitopis badionotus,*
like the African Bermudian women who
raised me up, digest detritus from marine

snow, absorb what is discarded from above,
but when stroked too much, throw up,
extrude parts, and re-form with a spine intact.

Water Witch

Like they slipped on the banana peel
now high up in the air, they skid,
skip, fly across South Shore waves.

No wonder they need only half of
a pair of wings, want to stay bound
to the sea, iron it out with a flat board.

The lone apostrophe hanging above
without its pair, not belonging, not
yet inside any quotable place, one with

closure. Sometimes the skier soars up
to escape all surfaces, then is ditched
down into the water, for such witching ways.

Shakespearean

We stare at the jaws of the white shark,
teeth sharp as cut diamonds for
a Harry Winston necklace.

They must have had their own
beauty, a shimmering tiara
in the dark silk of the undersea.

But we cannot look without
seeing ribbons of red, the un-packaged
human. Neither can we look

at its snare without remembering
the slaves harvesting bright jewels
in a dark pit in Africa. Beauty

and treachery so close, so
much a part of the ocean where
the lionfish, dazzling as

a sequined evening purse,
hordes and steals, floats
in with its Shakespearean collar.

Searching for the Bermuda Triangle

The divers flip backwards off the side
of the trawler, do a somersault in reverse
to enter a world where everything is upside

down. Men float though laden with gear,
search for a math equation's three sided
dimensions, simple as a first lesson in

Geometry, a tent a child draws. The boat
bounces sound waves off the bottom,
form a triangle like a compass swings

open to measure disaster's exactitude and
cruel edges. A mountain of evidence rises,
diagrams become cross-hatched with x's, like

an embroidery ring stretched tight to embellish.
The craft travels back, forth, a whale bellows
through the coral ocean for her calves. As

a vacuum cleaner's nuzzle sucks up,
sucks in all the contours, shapes of debris
scattered below, hidden in a seaweed carpet.

Bioluminescence

An Elegant Jelly floats solo,
lone lamp shade in a tenement house,
dangles from the ceiling, fish flit,
roaches scurry the floor below.

Crown Jellies cluster, a chandelier
in a grand room where seahorses
are attendant waiters, and a shark
in a tux floats quietly by, a handkerchief

folded up for a jacket pocket.
Purple Striped Jelly, a dinner bell
glows as it rings! Humboldt Squid,
with flashy side stripes, a rocket ascends.

Comb Jelly's beaded strands, the angel
wings for a child's play. The undersea
patched together with bright pinpoints
rough as an early map. I remember

Scorsese's film on the Rolling Stones
where he scrubbed them clean
with luminescence. Keith Richards
dropped cigarettes from his mouth

like losing teeth. Sparks in the deep
create contours, ripples, torches in
a cave. Flecks brighten like a school of
fries shimmer before a whale swallows.

Somewhere

The wave unrolls a flag on the beach,
indents the sand with loose boundaries.

The dark clouds gather haunches
above the sea, a hippopotamus squatting.

We all want to be somewhere, retain a sense
of home. I dive through tide's glassy

fist, feel it rise, curl, form an *A okay!*
as it turns towards land for the moment.

Nomenclature

How we fall asleep in our own dreaming,
but the tide makes a sound like a sail flaps
in the wind, pulls us out to sea. And what would

we do there? Watch whales spurt water, foamy
speech blurbs about the deep sea. Watch octopus
flail arms, a knot tries to come undone.

Watch reefs comb snags out of the sea.
Watch spotted eels and rays float to the surface
skittery as a kite off South Shore. Remember

a sea sponge's dark smoke, an underwater
furnace. The sea puddings with tapioca complexion,
cooked in light coming through aquamarine.

Admit we have no names for this world.
No nomenclature, sectioned like a family tree
hangs words from tips, empty nooses on gallows.

Quest ceque dit?

The bird I hear is not a kiskadee,
not chirping *Quest ceque dit?*
What are you saying? in French
or as Bermudians say: *How you sound?*

Kiskadee *is* its name, sounds like it.
Maybe semitropical light penetrates
disguise, although a robber's mask
attempts anonymity, the visors island

motorcyclists wear. Some round as
a speech blurb, a silent driver inhabits
while the bike blasts a presence as
it flies by. Oh, to announce whom

we are, by what we say! Words
fly away from mouth's concave
roost when tongue like an insistent
mother bird, pushes each out, off.

Mohs Surgery

I remember swimming underwater,
the sunlight piercing through
as if to spear the tropical fish.

When my dermatologist sews up
my lip, her needle pricks nerve endings,
like pieces of thread she pulls.

It hurts around my mouth
as the scar heals, hurts like
a hook pulling me in on a line.

She covers my face with a circular
white cloth, flat as a deflated life preserver,
or the rubber ring which seals a jar.

The surgery lamp scatters soft light
gently across my body, like a dandelion
I have blown on to make a wish.

Intraocular Pressure

My eye doctor shows me
how the pupil, like a bud
needs moisture. Mine
producing too much.

I think of my siblings
and I bored
in a hotel room in
America, filled balloons

with water, watched
them fly around, flopping
off of walls, the Bream
and Jacks on the dock

at Lower Ferry. I think
of how the eye fills with
the ocean, when one swims
undersea even though closed tight.

How it is shaken from lids
in drops, like irises, dotted
by the sun, the scales falling
when we came up onto dry land.

Too Much of a Metaphor

It is too much of a metaphor to use,
my FAO Scwartz baby doll, maybe
a Madame Alexander, her head
rolling off in my arms as I approach

Bermuda High School for Girls,
try not to be late just as my father
leaves in his Morris Minor, out of the
reach of my cries, as I ran after him,

want him to fix her, screw the
neck into the body, above the smocked
Liberty of London dress that May,
our maid had sewn early in the week.

Too much to ask from a poem, that
I work this into stanzas, make it more
interesting than life, me standing alone,
barely the size of the doll, with decapitated

parts. My teacher, Ms. Beattie coming
outside, bends down to suggest the Doll
Hospital in Hamilton, binds the head
back with tape, before the bell rings.

The Peril of Politeness

What is Shade?

A Haitian gardener plants palm trees on the Boston Common.
—The Boston Globe

Unless it slides down the curved
leaf of a shiny palm tree. Lands

on the ground in arced wings,
could fly about as it will. What

is it, unless the sun is handed
to you in a frayed green rag

like a loquat at a fruit stand
in the gardener's country Haiti.

What is seeding unless it is
whispered through hands,

sifted like coins carefully
spent, weighed in secret. What

is shade unless the scythe of
a wide frond cuts the afternoon

light open? What is a public garden
until immigrants see a home

country in the waves of green
rising, falling, a wide sea crossed.

Camel

Funny looking as any apparition
a desert mind could have, dune

coloured humps pitched like
tents on sticks. Curves slope

into the teapot's ceremonial
spout full of amber liquid.

Eyelids, lashes curl back from
the heat of flirting with the sun.

Lips large enough to drink water
from any blue and dry and dusty sky.

Bermuda Land Snail

It is handy to come with your own glue,
so you can adhere to anything while

your shell whirls like a hurricane center,
a spiral of action while you are so slow.

A kind of joke on you by nature, a ram's
horn with a fat awkward tongue. And to be

a tricycle of sorts, your feelers, rubbery
handlebars on a toddler's clumsy first ride.

A measuring tape to record our earliest
life, white body, surf rushing to find a shore.

The Perils of Politeness

As if manners might save one
from a precarious fate, motorists
in the West Country stare at one another
down along gorse, blackthorn and hawthorn

lined roads where one could say they
hedge bets on survival. Cowboys
at noon in the Wild West, or pistols at
dawn on a Country Estate, one learns

to drive right into headlights, the unblinking
eyes of a Morris Minor, Austin Healy, Hillman.
Hoping that like Abraham, God supplies
an alternative to a sacrifice in the bush.

But not one of the sheep peacefully grazing,
held in by such natural barriers, but rather
for a small space arced as a wing to the side,
a dent, as if one's fender was hit straight on.

A comma in this wily death sentence of a road,
last minute, and utterly presumed, as *Sorry!*
accompanies a wave, like a windshield
wiper clears the view from the dismal rain.

Flight Attendant

Kate could be her mother pushing
a refreshment cart down the central
isle of the plane as she wields Princess

Charlotte Elizabeth Diana through
the elderly British crowd, squatting under
umbrellas, like newly hatched chicks

in their pointy shells. Could be as she
serves them what they want. Hair neat as
a stewardess, nothing out of line. William

appearing, a captain straightening his tie,
as they briskly walk through waving,
smiling, assuring a turbulent free flight.

Cuba

The wide finned Chevys in fifties
turquoise, light green, patrol Havana,
relics of the American dream, steel

curves, flanks of metallic horses on
a merry go round. The front grill,
wide teeth, a comic image of

the squeezed dollar bill, tightened
into a grin. This comrade drives
a cab, has a monthly allotment,

a feedbag of rice. Puffs a cigar,
smoke wafts back to passengers like
a mane streaming from a full gallop.

Slinky

The circular wire with blade tips
like arrows, at first looks like a lasso
to bring in the wild roving bronco,
the horse fleeing constraint, fences.

Reminds me of the Slinky, I would
get from FAO Swartz, too many times.
This barricade surrounds a region
of Malta like one erected in Hungary

where many fled Hitler. I think
of how a refugee has to slink, slip, slide:
a shadow between boundaries to
find safety. I watch them form

a human wall in pastoral fields
they walk without a footpath.
The silver rings weave a light,
flash like coins paid to traffickers.

Form a tunnel in air, the underground
railroads in the Southern States,
the Calais to the Dover one,
the spiraling connection between countries.

Taps

for Springer Turner, Confederate Telegraph Operator

I like to think as Springer Turner
pressed down to *tap! tap!* a message,
he knew the weight of words,
the terse brevity of a warning
where silences between, *tap! tap!*

shapes urgency. I like to think
when I push my laptop's silent keys,
their cushy life of easy flow, I learn
to be succinct. Strike down only in
emergencies, when something said

is needed, not forget words can kill
or save a life, *tap! tap!* I like to think
as you did, *tap! tap!* out letters, I learn
from you to let sound carry meaning,
to let rhythms, *tap! tap!* course

through. I like to think when my
heart *taps! taps!* down the long
ribbon of veins, carries, deciphers
a genetic code, it is from you
tap! tap! I learned a love for words.

Zero vs Nought

Like Zorro sliced open the O,
a watermelon at a picnic.
So active, rhymes with hero,
full of the American zest.

Nought, what is not, no thing
when something ought
to be, has British propriety.
A no and an ought equals nought.

Plankton

Crime Scene

I can't go to the lake today,
flat and round as the hurricane's
eye which deadened all sound

through the casuarinas and
poincianna. Can't watch as
the maple releases leaves:

small boats sailed by children
in the Grand Basin Rond
at the Jardin des Tuleries, Paris.

Can't follow the road's yellow
ribbon divider circling water,
sections off an autumnal crime scene.

First Signs

Glad to be back before the foliage fills
out the bare dark lines of trees. Limbs
freeze into a colouring book page without
the verdant hues, like the Bermuda Activity
one I bought back for my great nephew.

How will he know to colour in shades
of turquoise water? Pink sand? Orange mango,
loquat, paw paw? Yellow kiskadee with
a black robber's mask? How did I learn to
be glad to see daylily leaves uncurl like

out of rollers, spurt of mechanical hair
growth on my dolly. See the brook curve
the green here, there, sections of toy railroad
tracks left on a carpet. How did I learn to notice
snowdrop's soft bite into grass, spring's first teeth?

The Country my Father Brought Me To

Had streets of gold, each autumn
leaves cobbled the roads with it.

And the Maple, Oak, were Pinatas
the branches beat to empty out loot.

Is a place where each tree re- invents
itself each fall according to what it

weathers. Always passes out island canary
five pounder notes to a Bermudian immigrant

like me. Each one I pocket, is a torn
off wing from a pair, half a valentine.

Flares

The long strips of flypaper hang
from the barn ceiling, petrified
tongues of lizards, rodents,
dinosaurs. Lightning flashes

with the velocity of catching
what is airborne. Sticky
as toffee candy, twirls with
honeyed light. Flies like crystal

earrings in the roll of a ribbon,
the wire filament inside
a bulb, wings, bits of glass
in the season of fractured

flares. Each tree sets off,
explodes, drains colour
to the ground, an electrical
charge fades in currents.

That Summer

Is a lake, still, not with waves except
the hills reflect the shape of, back down
into the water. The sharp keel on

a ship, slices through, or the curvaceous
lines of shadow, a jump rope twirls
light. Is a lake, not the ocean where

surf is a snail, leaves the shell of
the breaking tide, and clumsily
comes ashore. There is no drama

here of entering, just a walking in
as my dog pedals by me in the water
as if we were cycling on a country lane.

Turner

I just found out my grandmother was born
in Connecticut. The place where cradles,
are like coffins, hard, wooden stiff.

Not flouncy with lace as in the mother
country. Where curtains pulled admit
sun in a room like an act against privacy.

Not in South Carolina, where Turner
ancestors arrived and palm trees soften
breezes by the feathers in their caps.

Instead in a place where winter oaks
beat and rake the wind with hard branches,
send it to a corner, to keep it from fidgeting.

Plankton

Like a glob of seaweed adrift in
the ocean, my Irish Water Spaniel's
brown curly body is a cluster of
plankton in the lake's clear water.

Tides on the South Shore brought
bunches in: mats or snarls
each wave combed out of
the sea's luminous hair.

The beach was lined with
bunches, pubic growth in
the pink fleshy sand, smelled
of salt and of juices streaking.

Like a squirrel fish feeding
in semi tropical waters, I feed
on this ritual, on the dark
shape of memories wandering.

Whiplash

I could say the first yellow
in the spring willow
is just like the gold of

my dog peeing on white
snow which has turned
into boulders, cement blocks

outside my kitchen door.
I could say the seasons
whiplash back as the branch

drapes like a lariat spliced
into prongs of twine. I
could, but I see such

tentative owning, a timid
claim of space, the treacle,
leaking warmth into all

the frozen crevices winter's
wrinkly map has made
of the landscape like

AAA ones we toss on
the floor in our heated cars,
but can never fold back up.

Never arrange distances
back into oblong houses,
envelopes to send a season away.

Too Early

To make wishes, yet white dandelions show,
sugary lollypops above the green. Will disperse,
Fourth of July firecrackers burst, soft seed frays,
fritters away, lettuce moths slight as pencil

shavings. Yet, even blowing candles out takes
practice, so huff hard, puff away this artic flurry
of snow, wish back the sun's gangly mane,
rip-roaring through before August's robust end.

Times Squared

Falling in Love with My Father in the Snow

Because when we came to America
the landscape was black and white,
snow and dark bark like the blotted print of
the New York Times he read on Sundays.

Because he brought us here in January,
when sleet swept across the horizon
like a curtain to erase what I had
known before, the colours of an island.

Because when he held the steering wheel
in his hand, like a faucet he could turn off,
on, he was so happy as the traffic rushed
by in streams of water, he was so thirsty for.

Times Squared

The crystal ball ascends like a transparent
elevator on the side of the building.

It hangs there, a sparkling globe on
the tip of a lit skyscraper which stands

in a row of illuminated glass, the steel
towers bright as Christmas trees.

Billboards flash below in squares,
presents in a box. Time will drop its ball,

a woman releases water for a birth. Descends
in the furor of family members, try to see

its face up close. A star slowly falling,
fading in the black tunnel of night. In Sydney,

London and in Roma, firecrackers bloom
white in the sky, a dandelion wished on.

Some wriggle up like the lima bean experiment
I did at Bermuda High School. Put a seedling

in a jar of water in the closet, then watched
as it began to worm upwards, seek light.

Chess

I inverse the tops of the medicine bottles,
place pills in. Their different shapes remind
me of the West Indian woman walking
Front Street with a basket on her head,

bringing mangos, oranges, paw paws to
her family. The colours: pink, orange,
yellow in the pareo draped over thighs,
a map of a land full of sun. The white

pills, small moons shed light in the
dark routes of veins. Buttons which
will open up relief for arms, legs,
heart, lungs and free a mind of pain.

Containers on my kitchen counter
are like the police, caps, the protective
helmets, labels across, a chest shield.
I hope antibiotics hold the mob back,

the infection crowding the roads of
my body. I hope each vial will help
check disease. I pick them up, put them
down, move pieces in a game of chess.

Tissue Box

A resurrection of wings flap
above the boxy sepulcher.

A collar pulled up to shield
from a chilly wind, frilly white

as a cleric's worn in the mid
nineteenth century when one

might believe the devil left
the body in a sneeze. *God*

bless you! As one convulses,
leaks rubber cement drippings,

into a veil of tears. Drools
mucous from the mouth's

edges like Walrus tusks. Held
to the nose, the tissue mimics

a font of rushing snot. *God*
bless you! The world is tidied,

demons picked up lightly,
with a box of dainty Kleenex.

Compact

When friends flip out their
cell phones like lockets,
a clam shell shut tight,

I am reminded of how
women opened compacts
with the round terra firma

of makeup below and
the shimmering mirror
above full of heaven. I

watched as Stratford College
roommates powdered noses,
the circular pad at the tip

made us clowns. If we're
made from dust, here we
go again, remake ourselves

with Revlon's soft pink
granules as God's glassy eye
shines back at us from the top.

Scales

It glows at night like a moon, the round
face of the Salter weight machine next

to my bed. Hooded in white, as if in hiding, a monk
in a cloak full of meditation, winter's cold

facts. An Eskimo stares back at me, with chubby
cheeks. When I stand on the landing pad,

below the luminous circle, I feel my full
volume, no absence of gravity. A precise

arrow cuts into the shining circle like a sous
chef slices brie. I ripen in my skin, blue veins

surface. A slow melt downwards, pudgy to
touch. I think of the ancient English measure-

ment by stones as labourers built walls around
the girth of a private estate. I am a lumpy bag

of rocks. When I read my exact weight, scales
fall from eyes. I want to wax and to wane.

Hot Water Bottle

My laptop with a soft pink
cover may as well be a hot water
bottle I bring along. May

as well be a baby the airport
security officer hands me
with her see through gloves

as it comes out of the X ray
machine's long birth canal,
trails an umbilical cord.

Like the small Cover Girl
compact I opened, closed
at Stratford College when

my world was a small circle.
But bigger than when I flashed
light off mirrors to sailboats

passing on South Shore,
mimicked smugglers I read
about in Enid Blyton's Famous

Five. Twirled light like Gibbs
Hill Lighthouse in Southampton,
shafts spinning their helicopter

propellers. I see myself in Dell's
glassy oblong screen, the shape
of a rear view, pulls me into

a horizon while I pump letters
fast, fast. Push gas pedals to
the floor, and am lurched forward.

Morning Flight

It is not a hearse exactly,
as the black taxi beams
through the night, makes
a way through the curved

Bermuda lanes, to pick me
up. Not an out of body
experience exactly, as the radio
cab clicks in and out, with

locations, streets my memory
might scan near death,
now packs for the journey:
South Shore, Hamilton, Flatt's

Inlet. As if the driver turned
over in her sleep, mutters
details from a good day's
work. Not resurrection exactly

as the flight takes me up into
an even blue where turbulence
smooths out like rumpled clothes
in my baggage will after spin/dry.

After Sixty

It is all about eyebrows
my childhood friend says.
I sketch in dark black arcs
like a raven's spread wings.

Or are the double arches of
MacDonald's: we are both
selling meat. Two lines, one on
each side of my chin, gills on

Groupers, resemble knitting
needles trying to knit this
sorry rag of a mouth, where
lipstick doesn't so much bleed,

as is incapable of defining edges,
long blurred into skin, little lines
barely hold it in place. The stitches
I learned in sewing class at BHS.

Painted Woman

after Cecily Brown

Paint her in, seal the edges of her
bare body, drop paint on her, like
a sinker on a fishing line drowns

the hook. Make sure she can't
breathe, can barely turn to look at
you, her Master. I would rather

a woman paint another naked:
waves of high pink, choppy as
an ocean, push the frame's eddies.

The subject spread across the canvas:
the geography of acute sensations
a nude is when her skin is touched.

Jackson

Lassoes the canvas, twirls paint round, round,
a cowhand showing off. This painting

might buck, throw him. Better keep it on
the ground until it is ready to be branded,

bear his name. Each one a map of
the Wild West's changing terrain. Throws

colour, the way farmers spread grain for food,
all about chance feeding the masses. Topples

NYC's skyscrapers like dominoes,
a man need not climb up to find space.

Castanets

Her phone is rotary dial,
a sprocket in the middle,
holes for fingers around a center,
the earth with circling planets.

She rotates the numbers,
speeds them up to make
a connection. They add up to
the miles between her, her island.

The curved metal clip at
the wheel's cusp, to stop
the spinning, conversation's
last tooth, hangs full of a wisdom.

His, a cell, beak-ish, tight
castanets in his palm, turns
it towards the tree frogs'
night whistling, calls her back.

Lockets

Cousin Wendy tells me when we
grew up on Bermuda, we were like
mid twentieth century mutes in a Sea
Venture, caught between a rock or two.

I say *Yes! We let the ocean fill our ears, like
conches before we spoke.* Mutes in a mutiny
against linear language, the death walk
piracy plank of the horizon's flattened edge.

Sound curled our veins, the vines of Allamanda
trumpets clinging to limestone homes,
hung on with jump rope feet. Learned syntax
ebbed, flowed, brought in, out with petticoat

turns, the swish of a silk skirt, and yes!
left shells the tide broke through like lockets.
Mutes until words mutated, found
the norm to catch the cusp of circles,

Hurricane Emily's eye, her spheres,
and the returning silence from what is
spun out to edges, the clothes petal
softened from a constant cycle of wash.

Moon Gate

The moon gate on the property
of the Princess Hotel is
a circle set in cement,
protrudes at the top like
a wee diamond on a common

engagement ring. Better set in stone
this precarious moment,
the impossible arc that tumbles
without paste. Better set in
stone the honeymoon giddiness

with the tropical sea seen
through. The many waves
splashing like burst bubbles blown.
The horizon line halving the circle,
surf, the many veils the bride will adorn.

Yes! Yes! Yes!

Is what Cartier Bresson said
shooting in the streets
of Paris, before his Leica
decisively guillotines the moment.

Camera flashes throw
their brief illumination
over subjects, give them
wings to ascend, fly away.

The white light of dying
covers the deceased,
a sheet in a hospital,
tucks them into a sleep.

The circle of the lens,
a pale moon of death
pulls members into
the camera's casket.

Rocking the Fixer

It is what is not in the photograph
we respond to. The spaces in the island
landscape not built up, still full of palms,
cedars, oleanders. The sailboats in the

distance like a row of tents on the horizon,
or a line of Tibetan flags taut with the absence
in between. The sun blotchy as a streaked
darkroom chemical. I remember rocking

the fixer tray as images surface in a cradle,
a distorted swimmer comes to the top of
water in the harbour. The Westclox Timer
with numerals large as the ones used in

a nursery to teach a child to count.
The loud *Tick! Tock!* as if time is a wind
up toy, one can turn back, forward like
black and white film on sprockets in

my Leica. Capture, push the button
down, a thumb tack made of steel.
So the shutter unfolds its creased
wings like a raven, before it flies.

How to Dress for a Funeral

Wear a heavy heart. Wear tie
shoes, clumsy brogues to fasten
yourself to earth. The laces cross
back, forth stitch you in. Wear

a loose jacket, too big for your bones,
so you remain anonymous in your
body, childlike, as if you haven't
grown into the fit, death still

too big for you. May your pants
be blades, sharp as fenders
and your shirt white as heaven's
wings which you will need. Your

tie hanging down, forked as
a tongue noosing your mind,
two leaves part beneath a bud,
opens at night, blooms into a Cereus.

In your front pocket always have
a handkerchief, pyramid of a sail
death unfolded, where tears
are collected, too dear to lose.

Matisse's Cut Outs

It is more about what is cut away,
off, fat on a chop no longer needed.

The scissors, two fingers, a peace
sign made with what remains, left.

Do we need years looking, to see
a few shapes, believe authenticity?

Death simplifies: a life flashes, the reel
edited, what one should, has to know

before lights out. Can we be summed up?
A few forms, things define us. Like you,

we come to terms with what time
eats away, as the two blades gobble

up material: speech blurbs of too much
said fall to the side. The metal x marks

a spot of choice. The action of a swimmer's
legs kicking in a reel played backwards.

Un-Box

*They have taken away my Lord, and I do not know where they
have laid him*

—John20:2

Takes a woman to want to put
the man in a box, a keepsake
for all the good times as Mary
did when Christ died. Takes

a man to change on her, get
a new identity as Jesus did
when he came back. Said
don't hold onto me so he

could fly without limits. Takes
a great God to shake us up,
an earth cousin planet shows in
space, a Shooter to hit our Ringer.

Takes men in women's bodies
to mix it up, women in men's,
as we ponder transgender,
un-box our thoughts, ascend.

Bermuda Google Earth

I follow the yellow brick road,
see the Somerset Cricket Club,
Christ Church blur as if I'm on
my Mobylette, as if this line of

fire is memory's comet speeding
through. I am Dorothy, I can
click ! click! be in Kansas, be
where I want to be. Drive through

without spoiling the environment,
no fossil fuels. I saw the woman
hired by Google to track the island.
She was laden with equipment

like a 1950's tourist on an underwater
dive inside a glass bubble. *Which
way to town?* I say follow the bus
stop posts. The popsicles sticks'

melted colours: blue for to sky, to sea,
to where rain comes. Pink for to
the island's Tiddlywink belly button,
the soft limestone it is made up of.

About the Author

Nancy Anne Miller is a Bermudian poet with five books: *Somersault* (*Guernica Edition*), *Immigrant's Autumn* (Aldrich Press), *Because There Was No Sea* (Anaphora Literary Press), *Water Logged* (Aldrich Press), and *Star Map*. (Future Cycle Press). Her poems have appeared *in Edinburgh Review (UK)*, *Agenda (UK)*, *Ambit (UK)*, *Stand (UK)*, *The International Literary Quarterly (UK)*, *Magma (UK)*, *Journal of Postcolonial Writing (UK)*, *Mslexia (UK)*, *New Welsh Review (UK)*, *Wasafiri(UK)*, *The Moth (IE)*, *A New Ulster (IE)*, *Southword (IE)*, *The Fiddlehead (CA)*, *The Dalhousie Review (CA)*, *The Toronto Quarterly blog (CA)*, *Postcolonial Text (CA)*, *Transnational Literatures (AU)*, *The Caribbean Writer (VI)*, *tongues of the ocean (BS)*, *Sargasso: Journal of Caribbean Literature (PR)*, *Bim (BB)*, *Poui (BB)*, *Moko: Caribbean Arts and Letters (TT)*, *The Arts Journal (GY)* *The Pacuare Anthology (CR)*, *The Missing Slate (PK)*, *The Open Road Review (IN)*, *Poetry Salzburg Review (AT)*, *Proud Flesh: New Afrikan Journal of Culture, Politics, Consciousness USA)*, *Journal of Caribbean Literatures (USA)*, *St. Katherine's Review (USA)*, *Hampton Sydney Poetry Review(USA)*, *Theodate (USA)* *Free Verse: A Journal of Contemporary Poetry and Poetics* (USA), *Interviewing the Caribbean* (USA), among others. She has an M Litt in Creative Writing from Univ. of Glasgow, is a MacDowell Fellow, and is a three time recipient of Bermuda Art Council Grants. She represented Bermuda in Poetry World Cup and in 2009 organized Ber-Mused, a poetry reading for BDA's 400 th Anniversary. She was shortlisted for the small axe salon (Caribbean) poetry prize (2013), guest edited *tongues of the ocean (BS)*, and was included in *Arts Etc Barbados* (BB) tribute for Edward Kamau Brathwaite.

www.ingramcontent.com/pod-product-compliance
Lightning Source LLC
Chambersburg PA
CBHW071108090426
42737CB00013B/2540